I JUS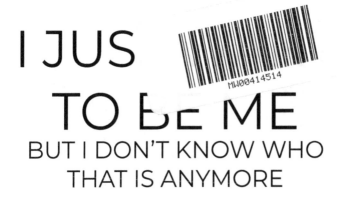
TO BE ME
BUT I DON'T KNOW WHO
THAT IS ANYMORE

FROM PEOPLE PLEASER TO PERSONAL TRUTH,
FINDING YOUR VOICE UNDER ALL THE NOISE.

LOVE, BOBBIE JO

May this book inspire you to be who you really are.
Love, Bobbie Jo

TABLE OF CONTENTS

FOREWARD

I believe that when we are born, we know who we are. There isn't anything we are trying to "be." We didn't learn how to please yet. We just simply, and beautifully, exist.

Then, as we grow, we start to learn what behaviors create what reactions and act in ways to create the ones we prefer. We listen to what we are told, as our little selves start getting molded by our families, friends and society. This carries on, usually unconsciously, into our adult years.

It is only when we reach a point of unhappiness and questioning, that we stop to take stock of what is really going on. A time when we ask ourselves, "Who Am I?"

In this book, I share my story with vulnerability and humor in a way to relate to others who may share similar experiences. I also encourage the reader to share reflections of their own on the blank spaces I've left throughout the book.

It is my hope that you find connection and inspiration, but most of all—that you find yourself.

Love, Bobbie Jo

CHAPTER

ONE

*It has been said "The World is Your Stage,"
however, it should also mention to choose
your parts wisely.*

STEPPING INTO ACT TWO

What Pleasing Taught Me: Applause for performing feels better from an actual stage.

I feel as if intermission just ended, and I am stepping into Act Two of my life.

Act One—I was the actress who desired to be cast. I auditioned for what I believed the director wanted, showed up religiously for rehearsals, memorized my lines, got in wardrobe, and followed the script.

I played my part, allowing my character to be shaped by the cues and other cast members. The audience's applause came when expectations were met. I was a good girl who played my part well.

Performances eventually became tiring, and the applause no longer mattered as much. Deep down, I knew my character was missing something. The opportunity to find it came at intermission.

"Intermission" was my body's way of yelling "CUT!" and pulling the curtain for a break.

During this pause, I felt as though I woke up, seeing myself beyond the "actor." It was time to break character. I tossed the script, took off the mask, let go of what everyone told me to be, and looked within, in search of who I really was.

Now, as the curtain pulls back, I walk unto the stage unscripted, un-molded, unmasked, real, raw, honest and vulnerable. It's like an improv where anything can happen, and I welcome it.

Is it scary? Yes. It's so much more comfortable to "know the script." But that's not real living. That's acting. And the girl who always dreamed of being an actress, is now ready to simply be the girl—no applause necessary, for she now knows true love and validation come from within.

And when it's time for the curtain call, she shall bow deeply—not for the roles she has played, but for the opportunity she was given to truly live.

I invite you to live your "act" out of character (or shall I say, in your true character). To simply embody the truth of who you are. To fully live—unscripted.

What I've Learned:

True living is more fulfilling than acting. Applause is just noise and does not define our value. We can easily slip into "roles" and "pleasing," therefore, being in touch with our true character is essential to staying "unscripted."

Your Turn to Reflect.

On the following lines (or in your journal), take a moment to reflect on who your "true character" really is. Is it the role you are currently playing? Are there any masks you are wearing, or parts you are playing that feel off character?

_____
_____
_____
_____
_____
_____
_____
_____
_____
_____
_____
_____
_____
_____
_____
_____
_____
_____
_____
_____
_____
_____
_____
_____
_____

CHAPTER

TWO

*I didn't want to lose you, so I
lost myself instead.*

LOST IN LOVE

*What Love Taught Me: Commit to knowing
yourself before committing
to another.*

Life Changes

I never had kids. The closest that I came was a miscarriage due to an unknown atopic pregnancy. It's amazing how maternal instinct kicks in; I wanted to do whatever I could to save that child I didn't even know I was carrying. Loss is hard, even when you didn't know you had something to lose.

A few years later, I met my husband. He already had three beautiful children. We discussed not having more, and I was okay with it. I never had that "clock" many of my friends had. You know, "At such and such an age I will be married with 2.5 kids living in a two-story home with a white picket fence." I was open to wherever life took me.

A part of me envisioned my little girl coming down the stairs in footie pajamas with a big smile on her face, excited to open her Christmas presents. An easy image to feel, as that was once me. There was also a part of me that thought my life could be spent as a single woman somehow making an impact on the world (doing so on a tropical isle of course!).

I didn't have it all drawn up like a beautiful, architectural image. It was more of a blank sheet of paper open to crayon markings wherever the Big Guy in the sky chose them to go. It's nice to be open like that, however, it's easy to lose yourself without a penciled-in sketch of preferences or boundaries in which you'd be okay with those markings going when you hand the crayons over.

In a very short amount of time, my life completely changed. I moved from the city to the country to live with my husband. This created a longer commute to my massage business, which in addition to lightening my client load due to a tiring body, eventually led to closing my doors.

I went from being a single dog-mom living in the city, to a married stepmom living in the country. I transitioned from being self-employed for 15 years, to once again working in a j-o-b. I went from holding the name I claimed for 39 years, to not only taking a new last name, but also losing my middle name due to a birth certificate error.

Roles and Boundaries

These changes were all about and for love. The struggle was that I didn't have or know my boundaries, nor what my "new role" was. I just handed the crayons over. I didn't make my dreams known or what expressions were vitally important to me, such as having my own business.

Looking back, it's no wonder I'd lose myself. Being a people pleaser at heart, and an "anything for love" girl, the crayons didn't have a box, but I felt myself allowing myself to be drawn into one.

I grasped to not lose myself, yet often struggled with how to make that happen and not disappoint those I loved. I tried to keep creative projects going on the side, mainly for self-expression. However, without my heart's full tending, I eventually grew tired and surrendered to being like most—simply going through the motions.

It's essential to know our MAP ("My Aligned Preferences") when we are "traveling" with another. To know our non-negotiable's. To express our deepest dreams and desires. When we put someone else fully in the drivers seat, with no sense of our own direction, it's easy to become lost.

What I've Learned:

When seeking love and approval from another, we can find ourselves doing things out of a place of pleasing, rather than being true to ourselves. While relationships require compromise and change, they also require us to know our own values and needs. It's an honoring of both our partner as well as ourself.

Your Turn to Reflect.

How is your commitment to yourself? Do you know your MAP? Your non-negotiable's? Have you made them clear to others? Are your boundaries in place?

_____

_____

_____

_____

_____

_____

_____

_____

_____

_____

_____

_____

_____

_____

_____

_____

_____

_____

_____

_____

_____

_____

_____

_____

_____

_____

_____

_____

_____

CHAPTER

THREE

I once thought I had forever,
and I ran around to please.
Then, I realized how brief I'm here,
and that brought me to my knees.
Now, I listen to my heart
and what it longs to express.
I honor its guidance more and more,
and I please less and less.

FROM HYSTERECTOMY TO WHOLE

What My Body Taught Me: You can literally lose a piece of yourself when you lose yourself.

The Body Speaks

Over a few years of trying to fit in a box, with its borders drawn tighter and tighter, I began experiencing health issues, and when I finally surrendered to the status quo, it hit the hardest. The word hysterectomy was brought up. I opted to try other options first.

I made the decision to not go back to the job I was at. This was something I had felt deep within earlier, even hearing my inner voice warning me, "If you go back, you will die." However, the people pleaser in me paused trying to figure out how to both honor myself and that inner knowing, as well as pleasing everyone else. Unfortunately, the two didn't mesh, and my decision was met with great unhappiness.

I focused on my health. I did what I could to try to heal myself—inner work, reading, educating myself, meditating, supplements, chiropractic care, energy healing, acupuncture—you name it, I tried it.

Healing is a Journey

After all I tried, I didn't heal physically, but I felt a healing on a deeper level, which gave me the peace of mind to move forward with medical assistance.

As I sat with my deep inner healing, yet lack of physical healing, I heard the message, "Be open to however the healing shows up."

Healing is more than we think it is. It has levels and layers—many ways it can show up. It's not always the outward appearance we think it is (or hope it will be). It's often an inner shift, a coming home to ourselves.

I truly believe all of this pre-healing helped with my surgery. I think I would have dealt with many more emotions if I didn't do them. It greatly helped prepare my body, mind and soul. I even used a guided meditation before, during (on headphones), and after surgery. There's a lot you can do to help your body, mind and spirit right alongside medical care.

The weeks I spent on the couch recovering from surgery, I immersed myself in my forgotten world. I watched every Wayne Dyer PBS special, read deep, insightful books, and even wrote a book myself.

Listening to Yourself

I listened "within" for my next step, which let me tell you, was not an easy task. I had a lot of pressure to get back to me—the me that wasn't me, but the person I was expected to be. When I thought about going through the motions again, something inside insisted "NO!"

I have to say, it's easy to listen to that inner voice when it aligns with all the outer voices. But when it is in contradiction to what others want for you—well, shit can really hit the fan!

It was a difficult place to be, but I'd ask myself, "How many pieces of yourself do you need to lose to learn?" One was enough. That voice I heard continues to be loud, and I have the deep knowing that there is no more time to fool around with "should" and "pleasing."

It's time to hand the crayons over to a Higher Power. It's time to be clear on those boundaries. It's time to honor the life I've been given—with deep love and respect for others too, don't get me wrong. It's learning new waters and how to navigate them, without tossing everyone out of the boat.

My hysterectomy was a wake-up call to get back to myself. This center of creativity and femininity that I abandoned first subtly whispered, then gently cried, until it knew it needed to scream to get my attention. And get my attention it did.

Its physical loss will not be in vain. The message is clear. It awoke me to finally share mine.

What I Learned:

The body speaks to us. Our pain, stress, and dis-ease all hold messages, if we learn to listen.

We start by simply becoming aware of our body, tuning into the subtle sensations, staying open and curious to the messages they bring.

Your Turn to Reflect.

Is there anything your body is saying to you now, or an "aha" from an earlier moment?

_____
_____
_____
_____
_____
_____
_____
_____
_____
_____
_____
_____
_____
_____
_____
_____
_____
_____
_____
_____
_____
_____
_____
_____
_____
_____
_____
_____
_____

CHAPTER

FOUR

*Children should be seen,
not heard.
Hush little baby, don't
say a word....*

HUSH MY CHILD

What Growing Up Taught Me: Innocence is a precious gift not to be silenced.

The Start of Self-Doubt

Where might we get our people pleasing traits, lack of self-trust or lack of confidence? For me, it unknowingly stemmed early, as most issues seem to.

A part of me could see these shadows I've carried, yet they really became highlighted when I was seeking healing to avoid my hysterectomy. A naturopathic chiropractor I saw used some amazing techniques. Before I get to the one that uncovered the depth of this discovery, I have to mention my "flatline."

I didn't experience a literal flatline, but when I was hooked up to a device that measured sympathetic and parasympathetic responses (our nervous system's "fight or flight" or "rest and digest" states), I had no change.

Whatever I did, my nervous system didn't respond. It didn't relax nor did it get excited, it just remained even. Now, I thought because I meditated it was a good thing— look how calm and consistent I could be! Yet, we need these things to function. The calm meditating was not the cause in this situation. My response was to the point that if a tiger walked into the room wanting to devour me, I would have simply sat there. It was as if I was flatlined—just like my inner voice had warned me, "you will die." I really started to understand. We can appear alive, but simply going through the motions is a dangerous, dangerous path.

When the chiropractor went on to "muscle-test" for different things, he would also test what age this emotion appeared in my life. For everything that came up, session after session, the same age would test—age eight. This revelation moved me to tears. I was eight years old when my brother unexpectedly passed away.

When he passed, a deep part of me knew he was okay—that I would see him again. Yet, I'd hear contradicting information, even from the church, stating that he may or may not be in Heaven because of his church attendance record.

As a kid, we trust adults as knowing more than us. Therefore, when I'd hear things that contradicted what I felt inside—well, I was just a kid so what did I know…

Using Your Voice

This time period is also when I spoke up to use my voice. When I returned to school after the funeral, I recall our class working on a crossword puzzle. My classmates were shouting out answers as they'd find them. Feeling into that childhood joy again and wanting to fit in, I enthusiastically shared when I found one too. That is when the teacher decided to put a halt to it, and I was the one who was hushed and scolded.

Another big childhood silencing I recall was in church. I remember being so proud that I knew the "Our Father" prayer, that when it came time to say it, I belted that baby out with pride! This church shouting was soon hushed, due to embarrassment I am sure. (This still makes me smile as I can picture myself doing it!)

The night my brother passed away, I was at a sleepover. And even though he no longer lived at home (he was 18 years my senior), I still felt it wouldn't have happened if I was home. I unknowingly took on a sense of responsibility that wasn't mine to carry.

To recap, for me, this is where I believe my people pleasing started to take root: believing other's truths were more accurate than mine—that my voice doesn't matter, and if I use it, it may be silenced or embarrass someone I love, and that it is all my fault. "What if I'm wrong? Or hushed? What will people think? What if I embarrass myself or those I love? Will everyone be safe?"

It all came down to not feeling enough and looking to find that enough-ness and approval outside of myself. A basic human need we all have is the longing for a sense of belonging; we all want to be loved and accepted.

Transformation is truly an "inside" job. Don't hush your inner voice. Trust its wisdom. Learn to listen to it again.

What I've Learned:

We're all doing the best we can. My childhood experiences were all created out of love—people trying to keep me safe and protected. We do what we feel is best in the moment, and it's shaped by what's been done before us. We can choose to repeat them or to allow them to empower us to choose differently now. Just because something was, doesn't mean it still has to be. I can forgive others as well as myself and then create from this place of love and acceptance of self with clear vision. This moment is all there is. The past may have shaped us and brought us here, but what we do with the now is what matters. My voice may have been hushed, but now I know its value.

Your Turn to Reflect.

Do you feel you are silencing part of your voice? Do you trust your inner knowing? Is there an "old story" you are ready to grow from and write a fresh chapter with this new perspective? Write YOUR story, from today on.

_____

_____

_____

_____

_____

_____

_____

_____

_____

_____

_____

_____

_____

_____

_____

_____

_____

_____

_____

_____

_____

_____

_____

_____

_____

_____

CHAPTER

FIVE

All pieces of a puzzle are needed to create the full picture.

PIECES OF ME

What My Life Experience Taught Me: True acceptance comes from yourself.

The Whole Puzzle

Just like a puzzle contains many pieces that must come together to create the image, you and I are made up of many different qualities, expressions and unique values that make us, us.

For example, I have a very comedic, silly persona. I also have a deeply reflective, life-pondering side. On top of that, I've got a sexy "Hey baby!" expression, right next to a hippy-mermaid "Peace, Love and Seashells" quality—just to name a few.

Growing up, I recall relationships that had "preferences" to which expression they'd like to be in company with. I'm sure you can guess many opting for the "sexy" me versus the comedian or hippy.

This partial-approval led me to hide certain aspects of myself, as I was afraid pieces of me would be rejected. Often, this felt like "performing" rather than really being.

If you think about it, this can occur in many scenarios—for example, "Show your professional side."

I truly believe we are here to be ALL of ourselves.

I love watching "The Masked Singer." I find it fascinating how these well-known celebrities feel liberated by the "mask" to express parts of themselves freely, without being boxed-in to what is typically expected of them. It moves me to tears to watch their beautiful essence and truth emerge in such a free, powerful way.

Boxed In

Why do we box-in, or box others in? To fit in. To be accepted. To receive love. To feel there is a certain order or predictable consistency. Yet, it's in that "box" that we can become stifled.

It can feel like something is missing when we don't express the fullness of our soul. When we go beyond the box with a gentle, loving allowing, letting all parts of ourselves to emerge, a peace resonates within as our truth unfolds.

What I've Learned:

We are multi-faceted like beautiful jewels, meant to sparkle and shine in many ways. A piece of a puzzle is just a piece, until it combines with all the other pieces to reveal the beautiful, full image.

Your Turn to Reflect.

What pieces of your puzzle are you honoring, and what ones are still in the box? How may you show the world your picture? How can you be your full puzzle?

_____
_____
_____
_____
_____
_____
_____
_____
_____
_____
_____
_____
_____
_____
_____
_____
_____
_____
_____
_____
_____
_____
_____
_____
_____
_____

CHAPTER
SIX

I wanted to be a dancer,
but was told I had no rhythm.
I wanted to be a singer,
but was told I sang off-key.
I wanted to be an artist,
but was told I couldn't draw.
Everything I wanted to be,
I was told I couldn't.
For, I always had a flaw.
Now that I'm older, I no longer care
about my lack of rhythm,
inability to sing on key
or about stick figures in question.
For all I want to be is ME.
Flaws and all.
For dancing brings me joy.
Singing lifts my spirits.
And drawing frees my mind.

WHAT SHOULD I BE WHEN I GROW UP

What Indecision Taught Me: If you hand your future over to another, don't expect fulfillment to follow.

Making Decisions

When you don't trust your voice, you certainly don't trust your decisions. So, when a major life decision is at hand, what do you do? Ask someone else of course!

I attended a four-year college because, for the first two years, you really don't have to decide much. The general education credits you need fill that timeframe. It was when those were up that you have to decide, "What will I major in?"

As a child, I loved acting and theater! I even recall signing yearbooks with messages and the thought that my signature was going to be worth something someday—you know, when I was famous! Bobbie Jo on the big screen!

However, when I made mention of this major, the responses I received were, "You'll never make it in that. You won't make any money in that field. You need to choose something else. Something practical."

I spent the night before my major needed to be declared on the phone with my friend, paging through the options asking her, "What do you see me being?" The final decision? Communications (with an Electronic Media emphasis of course!).

Feeling Off

It seemed a valid choice. I had great opportunities in the field. I worked in television, and then got a great salary position within an advertising agency. I had it all—right? That is, until the cubicle I was in started closing in on me, and the numbers I was working with as a media buyer were making my eyes cross. My soul sank.

A regular paycheck, benefits, a coveted position—why would anyone ever dream of leaving?—Because my soul leads my life (well, when I can hear it and actually listen). The people I worked with and for were great. I absolutely loved them all. However, I just couldn't do it anymore. When I reach this point, where my body, mind and soul say, "Enough!" there's no pushing through. It's hard to explain. I know many people who can (and who don't understand how I can't).

It's like there's this GPS (God's Plan Steering) that won't let me stay on a detour for long.

Like a bird on a wave, I was carried here and there to other jobs, until that inner voice guided me to kick my feet over to the next wave. One day, that wave was massage therapy.

This "calling" again was met with other's resistance, hearing how I wouldn't make any money "rubbing people's backs." My employer at the time even offered me a raise to stay and ignore this calling, but the soul, when it wants, speaks loud and clear.

Listening Outside

While I was empowered in making this change, it was short-lived, as I soon allowed the outer world to influence my decisions. In school, I was drawn to and fascinated by energy work. What intrigued me was the "invisible" level of healing, and working with our spiritual essence. However, when making mention of this to others, I heard, "No one gets that. You won't make any money. Deep tissue work is where it's at. That is what you must do to make it in this field." So, these little hands worked their asses off—well, if hands had asses. I became so depleted from over-giving that one day, I drove home to the wrong apartment.

Needless to say, my career path has been quite the journey! The times I've found the most fulfillment is when I honored that inner calling, that voice that "knows" the truth for me. That's the key—for YOU. Outside voices will always have opinions, and they can get us swimming in circles, ending up in places we'd rather not be.

What I've learned:

We are born with unique gifts and a purpose. They reside within us at all times, and we can change our course at any time to realign with them if we've steered away.

Your Turn to Reflect.

Are your decisions based on your calling or other's opinions? What calls to your heart and soul? What is within you wanting to be expressed? What's one small thing you can do today to live this?

_____

_____

_____

_____

_____

_____

_____

_____

_____

_____

_____

_____

_____

_____

_____

_____

_____

_____

_____

_____

_____

_____

_____

_____

_____

_____

CHAPTER

SEVEN

*Even in silence, the
sounds are loud.*

EVERYONE BE QUIET! I'M TRYING TO HEAR MYSELF

What Defiance Taught Me: You can't silence everyone around you without expecting them to shout.

The Price of Silence

The cost of listening to everyone else's voice but your own runs deep. When you finally realize how deep you got yourself, far away from yourself, it's hard to climb back up, especially when you still hear their voices and want to "please."

When the call of my own voice, and the need for pleasing myself, both became louder, I did what anyone in survival mode would do: silence the outside to save my soul. I guess after being hushed so much, it was my turn to hush.

I knew I'd eventually give in again if I listened, and be what everyone else wanted me to be. It was my life-story up to that point. Yet, that moment when my body said, "No more!" and I literally lost a piece of myself, I just couldn't go on in the same way.

Therefore, I put my head down and focused. Who was I? What did I want? What was my purpose? My gifts? My calling? My persona? My identity? My essence? My voice? My likes? My dislikes? My entire sense of self? How could one become so lost as to wonder who the F they are?

This period of questioning was great for getting clearer on who I really was, and what I aspired to be, as I started to feel again. I got back in touch with my soul (watching every Wayne Dyer PBS Special kind of does that!). However, it wasn't the best for relationships, as avoiding communication on certain matters doesn't land well.

It's not easy when you know your pattern and haven't yet built up the strength to choose your empowered truth. Yet in this space, as much as we'd like to, we can't shut the world out. We must keep living, communicating and connecting.

Without communication, rumination can occur. This is where the brain creates worse-case scenarios and plays them over and over in your mind, making them seem bigger and scarier with each showing. Eventually, it can convince you that the "movie" is true. When this false truth is believed, our actions are based on the movie and not reality.

We can hush the world only so long, just as we can only be hushed so long.

Everyone's voice matters. It's not about silencing any of them. It's about knowing so deeply that yours matters too, staying open to hearing others, and also being empowered to speak your personal truth.

What I've Learned:

Communication is key, even in difficult times. We are all a work in progress, and this life journey is about connection, both with ourselves and with others.

Often, things aren't what they seem; they are not nearly as bad. Check in if you're ruminating with a "movie" in your mind. Look only at the facts, not the "what-ifs."

When communication is difficult or feels unsafe, there are professionals who can step in and help. Therapists can hold a safe space for everyone to feel heard and seen and to help illuminate what is really going on so that your actions are based in a foundation of love and truth.

Your Turn to Reflect.

How do you feel about your communication, not only with others but with yourself? Do you feel you're living a life true to you, your honest expression and deepest calling?

_____
_____
_____
_____
_____
_____
_____
_____
_____
_____
_____
_____
_____
_____
_____
_____
_____
_____
_____
_____
_____
_____
_____
_____
_____

CHAPTER

EIGHT

*You can get lost in a sea of opinions
if you're not aware of
your very own.*

MIXED MESSAGES

What Reflecting Taught Me: The truth lies within you.

Act from Your Truth

We can receive a lot of contradictory information in life. If we are not clear within ourselves, it can cause us to question and swirl and get stuck. Reflecting on different scenarios in my life, I can see how I easily got confused.

I had relationships where my success wasn't always met with joy. There were a number of times where I'd be rejected when something good happened for me, eventually leading to my "playing small." I didn't want to lose the love, and patterns were showing me that if I was "too much" of anything, I would be left.

In life, we are taught that success, accomplishment and happiness are good things; however, in my personal relationships, I was experiencing something altogether different.

I JUST WANT TO BE ME

Therefore, when I was in a relationship where the opposite was true, it surely put me in a bind. The old thinking, "If I'm successful or too much, I'll lose love," to the new thinking, "If I'm not successful, I'll lose love." Well, shit! What's one to do?

Seek Within

This is life's greatest and constant lesson. It is WITHIN you. To not give our power away to receive acceptance and love, but to seek within to our own truth and act from there.

Everyone's definitions are different. What success is to one, is different to another. It's finding what it means for us and allowing that to lead. Everyone's values are different. Again, it's determining what our own values are and putting those in the driver's seat.

We can't make anyone else love us or accept us or tell us that we are enough. That is our job.

When I listen to my soul, my inner calling, it says, "Express yourself! Be Yourself!" When I listen to fear it says, "Please others." There's a big difference. Who are you listening to?

What I've Learned:

The only person that needs to love and accept you fully is YOU.

48

Your Turn to Reflect.

What is your definition of success? What are your opinions? What do you value? How can you love you more?

_____
_____
_____
_____
_____
_____
_____
_____
_____
_____
_____
_____
_____
_____
_____
_____
_____
_____
_____
_____
_____
_____
_____
_____
_____
_____
_____
_____
_____

CHAPTER

NINE

The truth to being in love,
is to love yourself more.
For if the one you love sets your value
you will feel broken when you
don't measure up.
If the one you love defines your beauty
you will feel defeated when
you don't fit the part.
If the one you love is your
source for love
you will feel empty when their
love isn't flowing
You must set your value.
You must define your beauty.
You must love you more.
Then, you can give and
accept love freely
for there is no need to be filled.
You are already valued,
beautiful and loved.
And no one can take that from you.

FROM THIS DAY FORWARD

What Healing Taught Me: You can start anew, just like the body that can heal itself.

Joy in the Journey

The beautiful thing about a journey is that you can always find the joy in it, if you look. JOurneY.

Just like the rain mixed with the sunshine creates a rainbow, the pain mixed with the pleasure creates a life worth living.

When I was a child, I wrote a poem foreshadowing my life path. It was entitled "Lost Dreams." It spoke about how you have a dream, yet you can lose it to another person's dream. You can become so lost as to wonder what your dream ever really was. Is it the one you're living? Or, are you trying to live a dream that someone else dreamt up for you?

We're allowed to change our minds, allowed to change course, allowed to make some turns on our path. The key is that you're not making those changes based on someone else's wishes.

Being Present

Being aware of each step you take is crucial, otherwise you may find yourself on a trail looking around wondering how in the world you even got there. It's about mindfully playing a role in your life. It may sound silly, but think about how many times you are driving and arrive at your destination and realize you don't even recall the drive.

Things, drives, lives can become mundane. When we do the same actions, drive the same roads, repeat the same patterns day after day, we can become in a daydream where we really aren't actively participating—physically, maybe, but not a whole lot more than that.

Those are the times it's easy to lose ourselves. We find ourselves doing things without really thinking about it, saying yes to commitments we'd rather say no to, doing things not in alignment with our values but because it's what everyone else is doing or what is expected of us. The list could go on and on.

By getting to know yourself again, knowing the path you want to aim for, the values in your heart, and checking in with these each step of your journey, you will find yourself in a much happier life. One you are present for. One you are co-creating. One you are proud of. And if you trip, like we all do, you are more compassionate and able to get back up and move forward, rather than continuing to fall over the same bump.

We can renew our path in so many ways. It can be making self-care and self-connection a priority. It could be switching careers. It can be a relationship transformation. The list goes on.

From this day forward, it's about making a new commitment to yourself. It's renewing your personal vows with yourself. It's making you and your wellbeing a priority.

It's making it known that your voice matters. It's knowing that you are enough! From this day forward, you show up as you. Authentic. Real. Raw. Honest. Bold. Because the world needs who YOU are.

What I've Learned:

You must choose yourself first. I know this contradicts much of what we may have been taught, but true compassion, love and service must first stem from within. We must be strong in who we are.

When you start with you, you will find more joy in life and healthier relationships too.

You are your purpose. Take a vow to yourself. Come back and renew that vow often.

Remember, this is a journey. A continuous journey. Be gentle with yourself.

I still catch myself "pleasing." I'm not perfect. I have moments where I notice I am looking outside for acceptance. There are times I am deeply insightful and others where my existence feels shallow. I'm spirit. I'm human. I'm always on a journey of balance, self-love, self-acceptance and true expression. I remind myself there is nothing to "find," only to "be." I know it. I say it. I follow it. I fuck up. I come back. I get frustrated. I forgive. I yell. I cry. I laugh. I love.

And that's what keeps me going—I love.

Your Turn to Reflect.

What is your vow to yourself?

_____
_____
_____
_____
_____
_____
_____
_____
_____
_____
_____
_____
_____
_____
_____
_____
_____
_____
_____
_____
_____
_____
_____
_____
_____
_____
_____
_____
_____

CHAPTER

TEN

The world tried to hide me underneath a heap of things. I thought I was lost, at times it seemed dark and unclear. Then a light peeked in, and I saw the way. Piece by piece, I removed what weighed me down, until a lightness of being and a brightness shining showed me I cannot be hid. No matter the layers, no matter the weight, I cannot be buried, for I am a light.

WHO ARE YOU?

What Searching Taught Me: You really can't lose yourself. You've been there all the while.

Feeling like you've lost yourself? As you've found out in this book, you are not alone. My story is just one of many. We all have our own, just as our journeys are unique.

The truth is, you're not really lost. It just feels like it. You're still there. There are just a few layers that got placed on top, making it hard to see yourself. All you have to do is uncover yourself, and you'll discover yourself. The you that's been there all the while.

Have some fun on the following pages to write your heart out. Let words, feelings, thoughts, ideas—whatever comes up—to flow out onto the paper. Reconnect with you. Allow your truth to emerge.

The world needs who YOU are—who you really are. Not the watered-down version. Not the version pleasing everyone else. The true you. The you that you came here to be.

ABOUT THE AUTHOR

Bobbie Jo loved writing ever since she was a child, yet only used her gift and passion for self expression and personalized gifts, as she listened to the voices of the "real world" and followed many different career paths.

Foreshadowed by a poem she wrote in her childhood entitled "Lost Dreams," she eventually found herself at a crossroads, looking within to once again find who she really was.

Writing called loudly to her, as that was the one thing that truly felt like home. Now, she uses her gift to share the words that flow through her in the form of inspirational writings and poetry, as well as healing and connecting guided meditations. Bobbie Jo also provides BodyMind Coaching to help others connect with their body wisdom to discover and live their true purpose. It is her passion and purpose to be a channel of love inspiring others in reclaiming and living those "lost dreams."

To discover more about Bobbie Jo, visit:

www.lovebobbiejo.com

CPSIA information can be obtained
at www.ICGtesting.com
Printed in the USA
LVHW050108231220
674889LV00015B/1454